Gulag #7

The Authorized Biography

Of

Karl Heinz Lawrenz

Charles B. Schwend

Quill To Book Publishing

Gulag #7

The Authorized Biography
Of
Karl Heinz Lawrence

Copyright 2018
By
Charles B. Schwend

Cover Copyright 2018
By
Charles B. Schwend

ISBN: 978-0-9966512-6-4
Published by
Quill To Book Publishing

All Rights reserved. This work may not be reproduced, stored or transferred in any form unless authorized by the author or publisher. Excerpts may be taken and used for reviews.

Charles Schwend

This work was taken from over one hundred hours of interview with Karl Heinz Lawrenz.

Any error of person or place is coincidental as it is from Karl H. Lawrenz's lifetime of memories.

Charles Schwend may be contacted at: www.charlesbschwend.com.

Quill To Book Publishing may be contacted at: www.quilltobookpub.com

Gulag #7 was previously published by Black Rose Writing in 2012

Gulag #7

Other Books Written by Charles Schwend

Dragon Dreams – A beautiful young woman; An intimidating old man; An ugly dragon; A mysterious sword; A mythology from the dawn of time. All challenge the sanity of an unwilling young sailor selected to become the leader of a secret organization that is over two thousand years old. While stationed at an old Kamikaze base, he saves an old man, with a secret life, from a frozen river. His valiant rescue empowers him by ancient mandate, to become the Master of the White Ninja, a position he does not understand, nor want. The story is a tapestry of myth, love, danger and death. Dragon Dreams will capture an open mind in a novel of historical fact and mythological accuracy. This is not a book of martial arts.

Charles Schwend

Words To Read, A Collection of Short Stories – A colorful, insightful, collection of 23 memoirs, stories and one poem, based on recollection, legend and fantasy. The writings stem from Schwend's experience in the U.S. Navy, hobbies, family, and observing the world around him. Fantasy and a vivid imagination provide the mental stimulation for the remaining words to entertain an inquisitive mind. The short stories are from true memoirs, observation, whimsical half truths to full out fictional whim.

Gulag #7, The Authorized Biography of Karl Lawrenz - A gritty account of Karl Lawrenz from birth in Pomerania, Germany to his current retirement as a U.S. Citizen, living in Highland, IL. This book is about his life and internment in a Siberian Gulag (POW camp) during WWII when he was 15 years old. He nearly died many times from starvation and illness. After WWII he continued to suffer under the harsh Russian rule of slave labor. He credits God for his life; his wife Inge, for the happiness found in his life; and the U.S. for the quality of his subsequent life. Some memories are a little grey. Karl cannot be one hundred percent sure that all his recall is without error. Some may not be remembered for a reason, or a purpose.

The Magical Switch – Originally written for a poetry contest sponsored by Famous Poets Institute and won an Honorable Mention from over seven thousand entries. The poem was written for a bedtime reading to assist young children to overcome their fear of sleeping in the dark. The book illustrations were made by Nicole Dormeier.

The Palace of Virtual Reality – A Professor Hamlock, head of a university science department, discovers how to bring holograms to life. Merlin the magician is the first to be recreated, followed by Aphrodite and other Greek Gods. Murder, lust, adventure and mystery soon follows.

The Keys - A collection of short stories that will entertain readers of every genre. Readers have acclaimed the stories as excellent reading. The Keys will be especially appreciated by readers that want to enjoy a short story, put the book down, and return at another time to start a new story.

Words, An Anthology of Short Writings - Editor of and Contributing Author.

Homemade Cordials, Better Than Bought - Homemade Cordials will enable the readers to successfully make a good quality cordial drink to their liking, with basic equipment. Anyone can make his or her own cordial that will rival anything bought.

Gulag #7

Dedication

This book is dedicated to my wife Dolores

GULAG #7

The Authorized Biography

Of

Karl Heinz Lawrenz

Gulag #7

Forward

Gulag: "Glavnoye Upravlyeniye Ispravityei'no-Trudovih Lagyeryer I koloniy" (The Chief Administrator of Corrective Labor Camps and Colonies): Run by the NKVD.

Gulag was not a term used officially within the U.S.S.R. Soviet system used terms like: Labor Camps; Re-education Camps; Prison Camps; P.O.W. Camps; Corrective Labor Camps, etc.

Many Russian concentration camps still exist today. This book is about one of the prisoners, Karl Heinz Lawrenz, during and after WWII. Karl is now a Naturalized U.S. Citizen, retired and living in Highland, Illinois, USA.

Karl was imprisoned at the young age of 15, in Gulags #1 and #7 of Siberia, just for being a German citizen. All the internees in his camp were displaced civilians. There were no criminal, political or military prisoners. He nearly died from starvation and illness many times. After

WWII was over, he continued to suffer under the harsh Russian rule of slave labor.

It was only by the grace of God, whom he credits for his life that he found his family who had also been searching for him. He credits his wife Inge for the happiness found in life and the United States for the quality of his subsequent life.

Some memories are a little grey. Karl cannot be one hundred percent sure that all his recall is without error. Some may not be remembered for a reason, or a purpose. To balance his story, Karl has provided some of the memories of his sister, Elfriede Kubeit, nee Lawrenz, that she wrote in her booklet "Memoirs of The Albert Lawrenz Family". At times the two perspectives of their accounts timelines overlap.

Acknowledgements

The author would like to acknowledge the terrible and the good memories of Karl Lawrenz. He suffered through the reliving of his harsh treatment while a prisoner in Siberia and later after being released, the hardships of just trying to stay alive, until returning to the fold of his family, while he was 15 and 16 years old. His emotional retelling of his experiences also remains in my memory.

Secondly, I would like to acknowledge the contribution of Karl's daughter, Karin and son-in-law Pat McMullen. I am not forgetting the exacting translation done by Karl's sister Linda and his brother in law, Mannfred Driesner.

The Highland League of Writers also contributed their critique and recommendations to the sporadic readings of this manuscript at our meetings.

And lastly, I am truly in debt to the readers as their opinion of this book is what really counts.

Without the readers, this book would not exist. Readers may also comment on the contents of this book by accessing my web site, **www.*charlesbschwend.com*.**

Charles "Chuck" Schwend

Chapter 1

Karl's Father, Albert Lawrenz as a young man

I was born Karl-Heinz Lawrenz, son of Albert and Margarete nee Czemper Lawrenz, on September 13, 1929 in Friedrichshuld, County of Rummelsburg, State Pomerania Germany. My father was a forest worker and born in our house on 24 December 1902, where I was also born. We later moved to Jannewitz in 1932, when I was 3. There we lived with my grandparents and my father's oldest brother, Herrmann. The new house had three rooms and a kitchen with an attached animal barn, but was not yet completed. A wooden barn and pigsty made up the out buildings. Our parents worked hard and long hours to make our new home livable. Building material was strewn about as construction was not yet complete. The farm was much larger than our previous home in Friedrichshuld and there was a great need for farm equipment and additional livestock. My parent's income never seemed to stretch to cover our needs. Mother cried often from worry. The children of our new neighbors quickly became friends with which we played. The land where I was a youth was fertile, produced heavy, and gave us abundant crops. During this time of heavy labor and building expansion, we experienced illnesses and accidents.

Karl's Parents:

Albert Lawrenz. DOB: 12-24-1902. DOD: 07-12-1992.

Margarete nee Czemper Lawrenz. DOB: 06-06-1908. DOD: 07-27-1988

On 12 April 1935 we got a new brother, Siegfried. Mother said "Good luck came with Siegfried." Grandmother helped mother with jobs she could do sitting down, like peeling potatoes. Grandfather and Hermann helped father with the outside work. Grandfather was also a certified cobbler and could repair anything made of leather. Harness, shoe or baskets, nothing was too hard for him to do. Father took on a second job as a horse trader. He bought two horses named "Lotte" and "Liese" to replace his first horses.

Elfriede came down with pneumonia and was admitted to the hospital in Schlawe, then in the summer of 1935 was sent to the island of "Sylt" for recovery. She lost six pounds in the first six weeks, but was quickly cured. In the fall Elfriede returned to school, and I became enrolled. We lived in the last house on the road "Varziner Weg" and since it was a thirty minutewalk, each way, we would play with our neighbors' children. Sometimes we would make snowmen, throw snowballs, or talk about what children think of. Sometimes some of the older boys would "wash the girls faces" with the snow. They did not like that much.

During periods of heavy snow, the main road would drift shut and we would sled with our German Shepherd dog Feldman pulling. Speeding down the hills on our sled was especially fun. Sledding always made the winter a little more enjoyable. We also wore our wooden shoes when outside in the winter. Sometimes we would try to ski on the wooden shoes, but that did not work very well and we would fall down on our back side. Sliding over the snow made our pants wet and many times would wear a hole in the fabric. We were scolded and sometimes punished. A spanking was easily forgotten, but being confined to our rooms was a terrible punishment.

Charles Schwend

Mother, sister Elfriede and I, Karl. 1930

Gulag #7

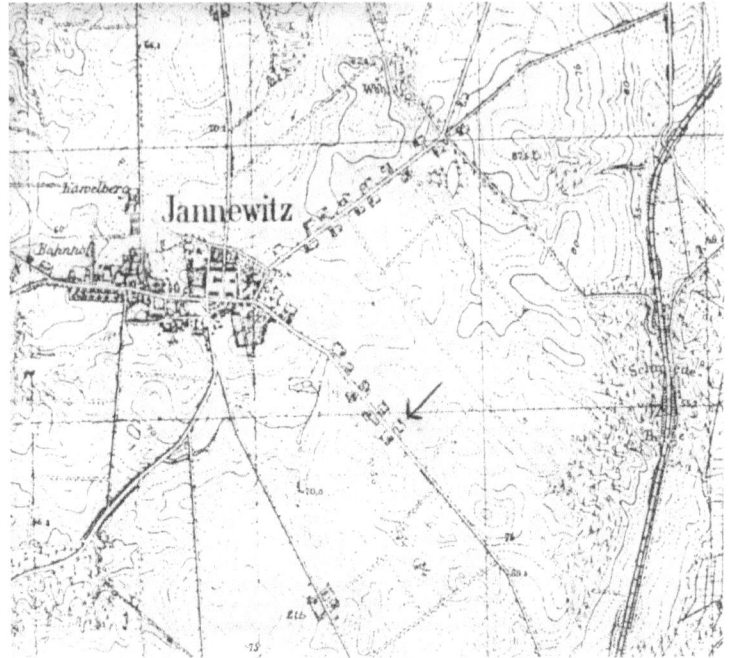

Our house was the last one on the right. (Indicated by arrow). Our school was located at Bahnhof, West of Jannewitz.

In the spring and summer, the forest to the East was full of blueberries, cranberries and mushrooms. My sister Eilfdrede and I, Karl, would pick the fruit and mushrooms to sell them by the baskets full.

Charles Schwend

The back of our house located in Friedrichshuld where I was born.

Now Poland owns all the land and tenant farmers till the poor soil they have created from poor land management. It is no longer fertile and no one there loves the land like we did, like a land owner does.

I have three sibling; sisters, Elfriede who is two years older than me; Gisela is 11 years younger and my brother Siegfried, who is six years younger than me. My paternal Grandparents also lived with us on a small eighty acre family farm where we enjoyed a good living and were content with our lives. We had two horses, six to eight cows, twenty pigs, twenty chickens, some rabbits, two turkeys, geese, ducks, and one goat. We raised potatoes, wheat, rye, barley, cabbage, beets (red beets for us and sugar beets for the animals) and an assortment of other vegetables. As little children, my parents expected us to help on the farm. Our starting chores were feeding the chickens, collecting the eggs and help clearing away the manure from behind the cattle. As we grew up, we started to help feeding and milking the cows, then taking care of the horses and pigs. We would collect the stones and rocks from the plowed land and put them in piles along the field. One of the adults would then carry them to one of the farm buildings.

Our out fields were also littered with small rocks and boulders lying just under the surface. We would gather them in the baskets Grandpa had made and make piles along the edge of the field. Papa would later load them onto his wagon and sell them for road construction. It was heavy work for Papa but the money earned money to purchase additional ground to farm.

One of these parcels, name Waldhoff, was located in the forest. We had to be very careful and protective of the crops, especially potatoes. The wild pigs would come out of the forest and dig up the ground to find the potatoes to eat. They would also rut out grain crops looking for food below the surface. Also in the forest was one special Beech tree where a swing was hung in a fork of a limb. We would climb to the top of the tree and was able to look out to see distant farms and other points of interest.

Feeding the goat was always a special chore. She had a peculiar way to thank you for feeding her. Whenever your back was turned, she would attempt to butt you in the rump. We all found ourselves face down to the ground on many occasions.

As I got older, I began to help in the fields, plowing, or following the harrow to broadcast crop seed. My brother and sisters would hoe weeds in the garden. Our hands and knees would become sore from the work. We would rather be playing and sometimes we would cry from the sore muscles and cracked skin on our hands. When the clover and hay ripened, it was cut and left in the field to dry. We use wooden rakes to turn the hay, several times, to ensure thorough drying before loading it onto a wagon. The hay would be taken to the barn and stored in a loft above the cow stalls.

Sometimes, especially when harvesting potatoes, Mother would have a bag of candy treats to pass out to us when we showed signed of fatigue or crankiness. We would take our lunch in the field. It was sometimes canned meat or other food that could be easily heated over a small fire and always tasted better outdoors than at home. Mother always made the luncheons feel more like we were on a picnic beneath two large oak trees.

In 1937, Siegfried now 2 ½ years old, started to play with the machinery in the field like he did in the barn. He crushed his left hand in the moving gears of the thrashing machine. I came to his help, reversing the gears to free his hand. We rushed Siegfried back home where grandmother rinsed his hand under cold water to stop the bleeding. I ran to the neighbors for help. They came by wagon to pick up Siegfried and take him to the hospital for treatment. At first they wanted to amputate his whole hand, and then decided only the thumb and index fingers would have to be removed to the first joints.

On January 26, 1938, our grandparents celebrated their Golden Anniversary. Everyone was present except Uncle Ernest and Marguerite

Lawrenz, who had immigrated to the United States in 1920 and settled in St Paul, Minnesota. Elfriede recited a poem, and then put a golden wreath on grandmother, while grandfather gave her a bouquet of flowers. Elfriede knew the poem by heart, but because off the excitement she could not remember it. She cried, but mother helped her finish the recital.

In 1939 our courtyard looked very different from the past. A wooden fence to protect it from the weather now surrounded it. A vegetable and flower garden was planted outside the fence, where it could be seen from the street. Mother was proud of her garden which flourished under her tending. A small fruit orchard and beds of berries were also planted to provide snacks and fruit through out the year. The flowers gave us enjoyment and peace after our work and on Sundays when we rested.

Father had also built on additions to the existing sheds and constructed a machine shed.

Grandpa used the shed for his repairs. The barn was sided with clapboards. Now our firewood would stay dry. Father had blueprints drawn up and material ordered for a new animal barn. Half of the supplies were already delivered when all new purchased material delivered was stopped for the war effort. The unused supplies were taken back and all plans for expansion came to a halt.

On 1 September 1939, war broke out against Poland. Papa was immediately drafted and sent to an engineering battalion near Posnia. The march into Poland did not last long and after a few weeks, Papa returned to the farm. As the war spread, Papa was worried again about the draft, but he was given a contract to provide wood shoring from his forest, for the coal mines. He was also driving trucks for Harfner-Bergbau, A.G. This contract temporarily exempted him from military service. One of our horses, Liese, was drafted into the military service. Papa was still worried for the running of our farm. Grandfather was too old and Karl too young.

Mother became ill with double pneumonia and the flu. Dr. Rorich had wanted to put her into a hospital but finally decided she could recover at home since we had taken care of our neighbor lady through her pneumonia recovery and we knew what to do. It was at this time Elfriede became knowledgeable about baking bread.

In the fall of 1940, Elfriede found out that Mother was pregnant. She had returned from town and left her shopping bag on the table. Elfriede looked into the bag and saw baby wash and other nursery things needed for a new baby. Early on Sunday, 24 November 1940 Mother came into our room to tell us to go to our neighbors, the Stuwes, to attend church with them. The mid-wife came to church with the news. The Pastor told the congregation from the pulpit that the Lawrenz family had a new baby girl, named Gisela. Elfriede was very happy. She had always wanted a sister. Now she could hardly wait for Gisela to grow big enough to play with.

Elfriede and I often fought and quarreled but Mother would always settle our differences with a hazelnut switch that she kept in a kitchen cabinet. I was now more careful about any outburst that might disturb our new sister. Elfriede always felt that she being the oldest was always blamed for the shenanigans that occurred.

Some wood and stones still remained from the new building plans. These were put to good use enlarging the barn and building a loft in the house that became Elfriede's room. The loft was the envy of all her friends.

Gisela was two and growing big. We would include her in our play. Elfriede was disappointed that she preferred to be with me and not her. Thereafter Elfriede seemed to become closer to Siegfried.

On 29 March 1942 Elfriede was confirmed. It was a beautiful winter day with heavy snow.

Gulag #7

We went to church on a horse drawn bell-sleigh. Now that she was confirmed, she could help me more in helping Papa.

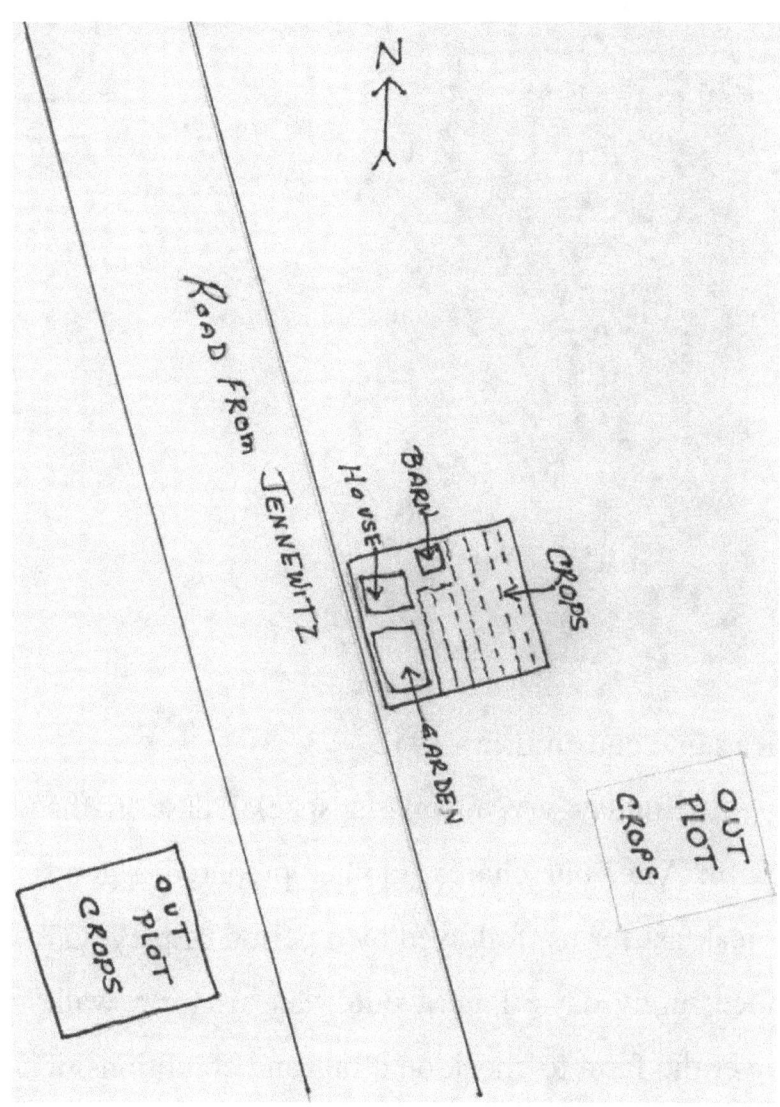

Gulag #7

Karl and cousin Eric - 1942

Sunday was always a special day on the farm. After our chores, mother prepared a good breakfast for us, followed by a period of play. On nice sunny days, Papa would take us for a walk over the farm to check on crops and conditions of the land. In late spring we would pick wild strawberries that grew on the nearby railroad embankment. These berries were sweeter than a girlfriend's kiss, or even a kiss from your grandmother. We would pick a gallon or so, take them home to clean and wash them. Mama would put the berries in our bowls and cover them with sweet cream for our special treat. You could not ask for a more delicious dessert.

My daily chores where feeding the livestock, mucking the barn, and cleaning the pig sty weekly. My sisters gathered eggs and fed the feathered fowl.

The cows and horses were kept in the barn, unless tethered out in grassy areas. They were not pastured. The hogs and pigs were kept in the sty and separated by age.

I would help broadcast crop seed and harvest crops with a piece of equipment called an "ableger". Elfriede and I would also help the neighboring farmers in their fields. We could keep our earned money and could spend it or add it to our bank savings. Even Gisela had her own savings book. We were taught from early on to be frugal.

Gulag #7

Papa had prospered and bought all the farm equipment we needed. Even our potato harvest now only lasted one week.

I have not seen a piece of machinery like that in the U.S. It would gather the shafted crops, cut and bundle then eject the sheaves out the back where they were stood upright in the field to finish drying. After drying, the bundles were taken to the barn for storage. Later in the winter we would thrash "dreschen" the grain.

Lawrenz family harvesting crops during WWII.
L – R Elfriede; Help hand; Dad; Mom; Karl.

The government to help out the neighboring farms, to harvest their shafted grain crops with our ableger, drafted me. My father was also ordered by the government to work on a second farm, helping a woman whose husband was drafted into the army. He had an extension on the government order to clear forest to make timbers for the coal mines to be used as bracing in the shaft and tunnels.

My girlfriend was in the German youth group called Bund Deutscher Maedchen "BDM". She was brought from south Germany to the North to help labor on the farms. We were both drafted for labor on the same farm. My father being drafted into the German Army did not keep me from this labor draft. I was fifteen years old and worked on the farm until the beginning of the Russian invasion. Usually one family male was left on a farm to work it.

Karl at age 15

Chapter 2

In the summer of 1942, the German army invaded Russia and advanced eastward toward Moscow and southeast to Stalingrad. In late 1943 the Russian army started a fiercely fought offensive West from Stalingrad. A short time later the German army started surrendering at Stalingrad after which it retreated. Hundreds of thousands were killed or captured.

Our school teacher gave a report every morning on the progress of the war. He reported to us that the Russian front was very cold this year. The German tanks and vehicles became bogged down in the deep snow and the engines froze up. The Russians were better adapted to this cold weather and slowly pushed the Germans back into Germany.

There was a Polish foreign laborer who worked at the paper factory in Hammermuhle that came to us asking for something to eat. Even though we were not allowed to give foodstuffs away for free, my mother gave him bread and lard. He was very thankful. Mother told him to return when she would bake bread. This man came again and again, and each time given food stuffs. One day he came and asked, "Madam, may I take off my rubber boots? My feet are burning so." His feet were bloody and wrapped in rags. Mother gave him a foot bath, powdered and bandaged his feet, then gave him new socks from my father. The man cried from sheer joy and wanted to kiss my mother's hands. He came back a few more times.

Soon all our teachers were drafted into the Army. The Lawrenz children, as well as our neighbors children became home schooled. We would have tests and attend special instructions at the school house, but most of these were nothing more than political nonsense.

My uncle Ernest mailed us a "care" package from the U.S. during the war. Somehow

I managed to remember his return address, just because of the unusualness of it. Little did I know how valuable this memory would become later in my life.

Mother liked to listen to music, so she bought me an accordion. I was supposed to learn to play it. Nothing helped me master the keys and rhythmic squeezing. I did learn that I did not have a talent for playing the accordion. Elfriede's friend Liechen did learn to play it and when she visited with us she would play the instrument accompanying our singing.

We did not know much about what was happening in the war, but did experience the shortages of everything. Grandpa, having a resourceful mind used old bicycle inner tubes to resole our shoes. He also made us "house shoes" called *schlurren* from heavy pieces of clothing and glue, with cobblers thread or pig gut.

Sometime in 1944 my father, Albert, was again drafted into the German army, leaving my grandfather and myself to tend the farm and livestock. We did not know he was captured by the allied forces and put into a prison camp. During the period of 1943 – 1944, all the large cities were heavily bombed. Elderly women and mothers with small children were sent to smaller villages and farms that were not yet bombed. A distant relative, Aunt Hanna Degner, with her parents and daughter came to live with us from Berlin, Butman St.

In the fall of 1944, there was a change in the war. Fugitives from East Prussia were fleeing the Eastern Front. They were trying to keep ahead of the advancing Russian Army and they spread horror stories of robbing, plundering, raping and even murder of women and children. The civilian population was taken into custody and transported back to Russia for forced labor.

The civilians were traveling in vehicles, horse and wagons, on foot or any mode of transportation available. All the roads were clogged with traffic. All were fleeing for their lives. I was drafted again for farm labor at some of the surrounding farms.

Mother's youngest sister Liesbeth was married on 11 January 1945 in Stolp. Her husband had been severely wounded in the war and was exempt from military service. All the relatives, that were able, attended. Despite the war, the ceremony and celebration was very comfortable. We received news that we too would have to flee soon from the invading Russians. We were given the address of mother's sister, Liesbeths Schucke and Mrs. Venslaaf, in Hagenow to go for safety.

A few days later, Dad received orders to report to the Volkssturm. All men and boys who could hold a rifle were drafted.

I returned home from my labor on the other farms because of Dad being drafted. We could hear the thunder of the big cannons in the distance. One morning, at dawn, late in January of 1945, a German Army officer informed us that we had to leave our home and property because our army was planning a defense against the advancing Russian army. They were going to build a barrier and a 'Panzer Graben', a ditch to protect the tanks from the advancing enemy.

We had a week to prepare our flight. We made a roof for the wagon out of blankets and rugs. Two horses were hitched to our wagon and we loaded only the most necessary items; meat, bread, canned goods, sausages and vegetables. Hay, barley and straw for the horses, were hung from the wagon top in back. We turned our livestock loose to forage on the land and left the barn door open, so they had access to their feed, until we could return. It was very difficult for all of us to lift my paralyzed grandmother onto the wagon, because she was unable to use her body from the waist down.

Russian planes were already dropping bombs on and around our farm. At night we could see fires reflected in the sky all around us. The cannons sounded like they were right outside our house. Near the end of February 1945, late in the afternoon, we left our farm, our destination unknown. By this time, the front was only a few kilometers from us. We could see the burning neighboring villages; we were cut off and nearly encircled by the Russians. Roadblocks and foxholes were everywhere. The only escape was towards the Baltic Sea. The order to escape was, "Flee in the direction of Gedanzk (Danzig). Leave there by boat going West." We were told to travel to the Northwest. This was the last time I ever saw our homeland. The roads and streets were covered with ice and snow. The horses slipped on the slick surface, so grandpa wrapped gunnysacks on their hoofs. Some of the livestock followed the line of wagons moving slowly on the road, or stood beside the road calling, in each their own way.

Gulag #7

Grandmother and Gisela were in the beds on the wagon. We were all wearing double clothing to keep ourselves warm as we walked beside the wagon. The horses were skittish from the sounds of war. On 5 March 1945, our flight began at the meeting place in the village. When all were assembled, we began our escape in the direction of Schlawe. The people of Lontow, Suchow and Quasdow were already underway. In Marienthal, Russian bullets were hitting the ground near the road we were on. In Pustamin we were able to finally rest.

People moving away before the invading Russian front.

After a week of traveling, everyone started to run out of hay for the horses. People started to steal the remaining hay. One morning an elderly grandmother died in one of the other wagons. The ground was frozen and not having time to properly bury her, she was wrapped with grain bags and quilts and carried in the hay on the back of the wagon. During the night, thieves took the hay, not realizing the elderly woman's body was inside.

We continued to travel in a generally northern direction, zig zaging around natural and military obstacles. We had traveled through our neighboring villages, the Russian advance just behind us. The roads were clogged with the fleeing refugees, stopping the entire line of evacuees. Wagons were lined up side by side. Everyone had to pull to the side of the road for the military convoys traveling in both directions. At one point Elfriede had to jump to the side to avoid being ran over by a German military vehicle but in the process was run over by our own wagon. We arrived at Kleingarde and it was about this time, 8 March 1945 that the advancing Russians overtook and captured us. At first we were glad because the idea of fleeing at this point seemed futile.

We had stayed overnight in a vacant private residence. Our horses were tethered in an outbuilding. Grandmother's crutch had broken and a temporary fix was attempted but that did not really work. We heard shooting and explosions in the distance. Suddenly, we heard shouts, "The Russians are here." My sister Elfriede and I looked outside through the window. We saw the advancing Russian foot soldiers shoot into the trees and German soldiers fall from them. Soon the door was kicked in and my mother was crying in fear of our lives. At first the Russians told everyone to bring them our clocks and watches. Word spread like wildfire that a few Germans had been shot because they would not surrender their watches. Then they wanted "Watca". My mother thought they were asking for sausage and told me, "Take them to our wagon and give them some sausages." One of the soldiers followed me. He took the sausage link and broke it in half. Sniffing and tasting, he said it was good. Later we found out that what they really wanted was Vodka. Later we heard

Gulag #7

that the Russians were shooting anyone that did not do what they ordered.

In the morning we were told we could go home. Hitching the horses to our wagon, we started the journey home. Dead bodies littered the countryside. Clothing was strewn everywhere. Deserted wagons had been plundered and dead livestock littered the edges of the road. On the road we were diverted to a field road to allow a military convoy full access to the road. Our new route took us down a steep hill and the wooden wagon tongue hit a frozen mound of dirt, breaking it. Another tongue was found but before we could leave, the Russians came and hassled me, hitting me. Grandfather decided that now was the time to turn over his watch, hoping that the gesture would allow us to continue back home. The Russians immediately confiscated our horses, leaving us with our wagon, supplies and paralyzed grandmother. The soldiers told me to take the horses to a military encampment at a nearby farm where I was told to stay for further orders. They wanted the horses to ride or pull supply wagons. When the soldiers were not looking, I snuck behind some heavy brush and made my way back to my family and told them what had happened. A small Russian pony had smelled the oats hanging from our wagon and had been following us. We hitched him to our wagon but found he could not pull it, he was too small.

Chapter 3

My mother recognized a neighbor woman, pushing a bicycle laden with luggage and carrying a small boy. My mother told me to go with her and return home. Hopefully I would not be capture there and could care for the livestock until she returned with our family when she could find transportation. I tagged along with the woman and her son, walking home.

Elfriede wrote in her memoirs, that Mother, Gisela, Siegfried and herself found a nearby farmer that agreed to put them up in his barn. He promised that he would find transportation for them and took them with their possessions to his bard. His house was already overfilled with the elderly that could not continue their travel.

The next morning they each packed a backpack with clothing and necessary utensils, unloaded their bicycles from the wagon, and tied the bed, with grandmother, to the small pony to trek back to their farm. Gisela was only about 4 ½ years old and we had to stop frequently as she easily tired.

The following day, a farmer they knew from a different town, overtook them with a wagon and team of horses that he had stolen from the Russians. He offered to take Grandmother, Grandfather and Gisela and much of their luggage. We followed along side. This arrangement was more comfortable with them, but ended when they came to a barricade where all horses were confiscated. Once again they were on foot with their bicycles and the pony. The wagon was abandoned by the side of the road with many others. Franz Kruggel happened to pass by and offered to take our grandparents and Gisela with them back to Jannewitz.

They left much of their luggage at the blacksmith in the village of Pustamin and traveling became a little easier. They quickly tired from exhaustion and lack of food. They met some returning repatriates that told them that all boys and young people were being captured around the village of Schlawe. They avoided Schlawe and stayed the night at an isolated farm. The farmer told them of an old dirt road that bypassed Schlawe and would take them to the village of Marienthal. Approaching Marienthal, they found that the Russians there were also taking all boy and young people. They stopped and returned to the secluded farm to stay overnight. The next morning the farmer told them of another dirt road that lead to the village of Quasdow. The road was nothing more than a field road, and in many places, they had to cross fields and locate another field road to follow.

They came to the Wipper river but the bridge was destroyed, down in the water. They left the bicycles and crossed the river with their belongings on the pony. They made their way to a road on the far side of Quasdow where a Russian vehicle overtook them and they motioned for Elfriede to come to the car. They acted ignorant, like they did not understand, and after a few attempts to get Elfriede to the car, left.

Arriving at Franz Kruggel's house in Hohernzollerdorf, they found Grandmother and Gisela. Grandfather was already at home with their belongings, settled in. The livestock was rounded up and returned to their barn. The house was in shambles as the doors were left open and animals took refuge inside. Everything was covered with and inch of dust, dirt, food scraps and broken glass. The plumbing was ruined from freezing and snow had blown in. We had to melt snow for wash water to clean up the mess.

The animals were relieved at their return, talking to them in their own way. The neighbors also made it back to their own farm. Only I did not return. The day after their return, they received word that I had been captured, but no other information was available.

Gulag #7

They Russians repeatedly searched the house for clocks, weapons and girls. Grandmother and Grandfather stayed in the house, but mother and the girls slept in the hay in the barn to avoid the soldiers. Mother and the girls had to keep constant vigilance during the day to avoid the searching soldiers and get to their hiding places. They heard of many girls and women, who did not have enough warning time to reach their hiding places, being raped, tortured and maltreated. They had to endure their tormentors time and time again.

Each farm house was assigned fugitive occupants by the Russians. They were assigned a family of six with their wagon and horses. The occupants lived on potatoes. The fugitives had nothing but the clothing on their backs. The mother of the family had no skirt and the baby no clothes. A skirt was provided by Elfriede and the baby received outgrown clothes from Gisela. The Russian soldiers were still a threat to the girls;

they hid themselves in the hay behind the pigsty. This was all new to the city girls. They hid themselves for several weeks until the family left.

Again and again the Russian soldiers would search the farms, looking for hard boiled eggs, clocks, weapons, and always "where are the girls?" The ground and straw was searched with bayonets. Their next assigned occupant was a Mrs. Febert from East Prussia. She could speak Russian and Polish, and would interpret for the family. All our livestock and fowl were confiscated and herded away. Somehow Mother and Grandfather managed to hide a pig and a few chickens that the Russians did not find. A few of the villagers were conscripted to herd the animals and they were never heard from again.

Grandpa was able to make a harness for the little Russian pony. It was old but readily pulled a small wagon. A "honey wagon", that was used to spread manure was sanitized, mounted on the small wagon, and put into service hauling water from the village pump to the farm.

On Easter Sunday we discovered a few loose cows. Lieschen, Siegfried and Elfriede herded them into the backyard. There were two milk cows, a pregnant young cow and three medium sized calves. The Krause's, our neighbor, took one cow, another went to the Biras' and the pregnant cow was kept at our farm. We now had milk and when the calves were butchered, we had fresh meat.

Papa had previously buried his collection of rifles in the machine shed, mostly home made and Mother was fearful of what would happen it they were found. Elfriede and Mother dug them up and threw them into the septic tank.

Food was become scarce at home. The local merchant helped when she could with soap, cleaning supplies, flour and food in exchange for rye. A neighbor took in the rye and returned with the bartered supplies in his old wagon. Salt was especially scarce. If an ox was slaughtered, it was shared throughout the neighborhood. Brine was used over and over. Even road salt was used as food grade. Some even tried to get the salt out of fertilizer. Mother made soap from boiled bones and meat scraps.

The cows still gave milk and Mother distributed the milk to neighbors with babies and small children, but kept most of the cream to make butter. At the end of May 1945 Mother and the children were assigned to work duties on other farms. The work group was supervised by three Serbs, two Polish and led by two Russians. Their first duty was to clean rutabagas and potatoes that were collected from everywhere, and place them into a silo. Then they thrashed grain and worked in the cow barn, milking, mucking stalls and maintaining cleanliness.

Their work day began at 5:00 a.m. and ended around 8: p.m. They usually were with the cows, when put out to pasture, to guard them from cattle thieves, herding them with willow whips. When the cows were brought back in for milking we were allowed to keep a little skimmed milk. Once in a while a cow was slaughtered and the workers were given a little meat. Each week a pound of flour was rationed out to them. Elfriede injured her hand between two fingers and the milking prevented healing. The wound would break open at every milking. This open cut remained with Elfriede through the fall harvest.

The machinery used at harvest came from the surrounding area. Any remaining horses were pressed into service pulling the machinery and wagons at least twice a week for the Russians. Any extra horses were taken to a collective farm to pull.

When it came time to rake the fields to dry the crops, Elfriede's hand became worse, but she still worked with one hand. One of the Serb farmhands, named Peter, helped finish her raking. Then she had to fetch brook water for the workers to drink. The next morning a red stripe ran from her fingers up past the elbow. She could no longer work with the blood poisoning. Mother bathed her arm with rubbing alcohol and showed to the Russian in charge who took her off the work detail for a few days. The blood poisoning left but the cut between Elfriede's fingers became infected, pussy and had a rotten smell. Mother treated the infection with a little sugar and the injury slowly healed.

Elfriede returned to a light duty work schedule, starting with house duties, then to light field work on our farm, then finally back to the hard labor on the collective farm. The fall harvest reached the peak work period and everyone raced to harvest the most grain. The neighboring Hanni family from Hohernzollerdorf brought in the largest harvest.

There was a turn-over of people living with the family on the farm. The Polish families were assigned to co-occupy the farms they were to

Gulag #7

eventually take over. They were demanding and very bossy. Clothing was scare for the Lawrenz family as most were left on the abandoned wagon.

Chapter 4

While Mother and the other children were struggling with the problems on the farm, the woman and child I was with, were coming to the city of Schlawe. We were about 15 KM from our farm. A barricade across the road stopped us. I was carrying her small boy. The woman was told to go left to a group of captured civilians and I was told to go right. When I reached the group to the right, a guard asked me where the small boy's mother was. I pointed to her in the other group. He told me to take the boy to his mother and return, which I did. The Russian soldiers put me with the group of male civilians. I had a wallet with a photograph of my girlfriend, I.D. and about m300 marks. They took my wallet, and everything else I had, from me and threw it into a fire. I am sure they kept the m300 marks. Up to this point, that was the worst thing that had happened to me. To see the photograph of my first love, go up in flames, was heart wrenching.

All male and female civilians captured, from age of about ten to sixty years old, were subjected to very inhumane treatment. We were kicked, pushed, called Nazi pigs, cursed and some left dead in ditches along the road if we faltered, fell or failed to follow orders. Civilians, under ten and over sixty, were not considered a threat to the Russians, or unsuitable for hard labor. The morning following our capture was cold and wet. It was springtime. We were lined up four across, counted, and ordered to march to the Polish border. We were told to not step out of line under threat of being shot. When vehicles approached, we were ordered to the side of the road to allow the traffic to pass. During our rest periods, we had to sit on the ground. If anyone stood, the guards would shoot over our heads. We were about one hundred prisoners, guarded at times with only four soldiers. Our meals, during the forced march of 40 to 45 kilometers toward the Polish border, consisted of a kind of soup morning and evening. At night we were allowed to rest in old barns or houses, if available.

During our forced march, we encountered totally burned out villages. Bodies in ditches, wagons turned over and dead animals. In one village we saw burnt bodies twisting up from muscle contraction in buildings still aflame. At night I still see the dreaded scenes, but not as much now as before. Every morning after eating, a guard with a few prisoners went ahead to find and prepare a site for the evening meal and sleeping. They traveled in a kitchen wagon. They prepared two meals a day, a warm soup prepared in kettles, and we drank from tin cans. The wagon carried all the cooking utensils and food supplies.

During the nights, two to four Russian Soldiers would select two or more women to rape. The women would be ordered to follow them for questioning. One morning, when we were lined up on the road for counting, a woman started crying and complained to the Russian officer of being gang raped. I saw her return the night before, crying and blood running down her legs. Some of the other prisoners encouraged her to report the brutal rape. She was in tears and hesitantly told the officer. He asked her if she could identify the rapists. "Yes" she replied. He lined up the guards and had her point out her attackers. She pointed to four of them. The officer stood one of the guilty four in front of our group, telling him "Turn around. This is what we do with traitors," and shot him in the back of the neck with a pistol, pushing his body into the ditch along the road. We were astonished that something like this was done. All rape attempts stopped. Our minds were numb from the way we were treated. Feelings – I don't remember any feelings. We were mindless, following what we were told to do, without reasoning or questioning.

After we marched to Poland, we joined others and were boarded into Polish railroad boxcars, women in one and men in the other, and like the Russian rail system, were smaller in capacity and rail gauge than the German rail system. Eighty people were packed into each boxcar with little food and water. Our food during the journey was "Kneckerbrot", dried roasted white bread that was given to us in a small bag. A bucket of unclean water was also provided. A hole, about 5"X8" was in the boxcar floor, on the opposite side from the locked side door. With no privacy, this was our latrine. Many people came down with diarrhea and other illnesses, leading to their death. The dead bodies were summarily thrown from the train to lie in ditches along the tracks where the wolves and wild animals feasted. Possessions of the dead were previously confiscated and their clothing was not decent enough to use.

When passing the Ural Mountains, we could not see the sun unless there was a break in the mountain peaks. Ice built up on the inside walls of the box cars. Some of the prisoners broke off chunks of ice to melt in their mouths. We were never given enough water to drink. I think this ice was contaminated and caused additional illness that lead to some of the deaths from the diarrhea and pneumonia.

Once during our transport, the train stopped at an open field, beside a drainage ditch about 3' wide and 1' deep, to wash ourselves, splashing the water over ourselves with our hands. Some of the detainees drank the polluted water, became sick with diarrhea, then pneumonia, and then more would die. A grassy prairie stretched out for as far as we could see. On the way to Siberia, one of my best friends lay next to me during the night. The next morning I found him dead when trying to wake him. "No luck." He would never wake up again, and became another face to remove from my memory. At the next stop at an open field, the guard came and pulled him off with the rest of the dead, throwing them into the ditch alongside the track.

I became very ill at the end of the trip. After five weeks of the primitive traveling, we arrived. I needed help to walk into the prison camp #1, near PravDinsk in Gor'ky Oblast, Siberia. The men and women were again separated. We had to sleep on the ground for the first night. It rained so hard, I thought the water would float us away. The next morning we found ourselves lying in inches of mud and water. Ditches were dug to divert the runoff, coming down the hill. A canvas fly was also put up to protect us from the weather.

That morning, the first morning I saw the sun shine, I woke up weak, vomiting and not breathing well. I was put into a hospital for rest and recuperation. After a short period of time, I was returned to my group of prisoners. We were

Gulag #7

interrogated day and night. Sitting under bright lights we were questioned "Did you or someone you know here in camp kill or think of killing Russian Soldiers?" or "Did you or someone you know here in camp ever mistreat Russian People?" We were never promised anything for telling them what they wanted to hear. They just beat us if we hesitated to answer their questions. The interrogations and unclean conditions made for miserable living. If the KGB interrogators did not like our replies, or our refusal to answer, we were beaten with rifle butts. On occasion, my ribs were bruised, or even cracked, from being hit with the rifle butts. We were told that we could never return to our homes because our land was nationalized for the Polish people.

400 plus people died on the train to camp #1. 700 arrived alive and one-third died while in camp #1. Our numbers decreased from the interrogations and beatings. The remaining people were taken to Prison Camp #7, to join

other prisoners, also separated by gender. One third of the prisoners in camp #7 had previously died and created the vacancies for us.

Gulag #7

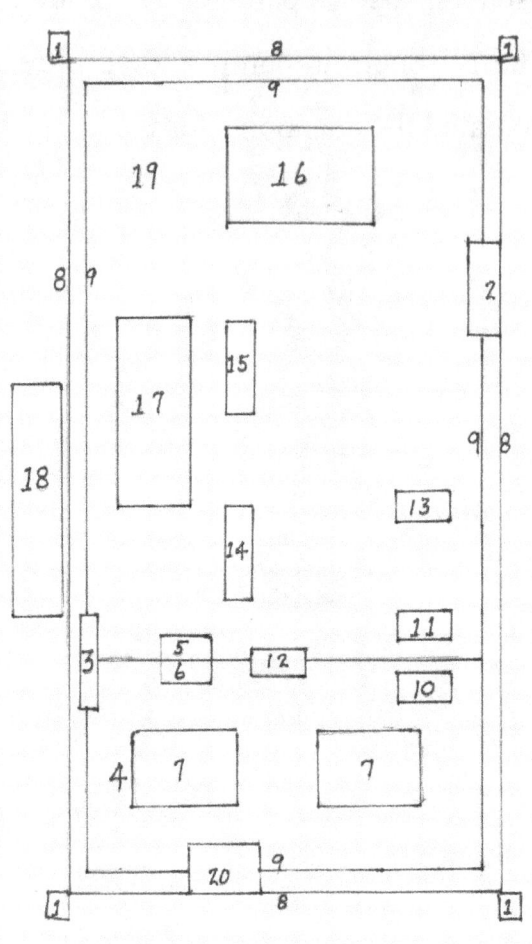

1 – Four Guard Towers.

2 – Main Gate.

3 – Side Gate.

4 – Women's Side of Camp.

5 – Man's Latrine.

6 – Women's Latrine.

7 – Women's Barracks.

8 – Electric Fence.

9 – Inner Fence.

10- Dead Women's Bunker.

11- Dead Men's Bunker.

12- Inside Gate between Men's/Women's Camps

13- Discipline "Punishment" Bunker.

14- Steam Building.

15- Sauna (Bading).

16- Men's Barracks.

17- Men's Barracks Where I Slept.

18- Guard's Barracks and Commissary.

19- Men's Camp.

20- Women's Camp

On entering prison camp #7, we were lined up just inside the main gate. There we were recounted and our name verified. We removed our clothes, coiled out belt and stuffed them into our shoes and marched naked to a sauna building where we put our clothes into a steam chamber for sanitizing. The next station was the sauna room where we too were steamed to clean us of parasites and bugs. The following station was cold showers to rinse off the dirt the steam pushed from our skin pores. The final step was the return of our now dry clothes for dressing. Following that day, and every day thereafter, we were counted and names tallied just inside the main gate. Our names were called and we answered with "Da", in a loud voice.

About every three weeks we had to repeat the sauna process of cleaning our bodies and clothes. If not for the sauna, we would have been able to grow mushrooms on our bodies. We welcomed the sauna process that made us feel fresh and invigorated. The sauna was located on the men's side of the camp and on occasion we would see the women lined up and running to the sauna with no clothes on. We took any enjoyment we could find, quite eagerly. Usually this view was seen from the window of our barracks. The scene was followed by pleasurable dreams on those nights.

I heard an unsubstantiated story, about a mother who clutched her ten year old boy to herself when she was captured. She refused to leave or become separated from him. "You can maim or kill me, or anything else, but I will not leave my son," she said.

The Russian Officer present said "Karashow (O.K.)" and allowed the boy to accompany his mother. After they were interned in Prison Camp #7, the circumstances about her capture circulated throughout the camp rapidly. We heard that the Russian guards and other prisoners gave the boy extra rations and preferential treatment. I never heard anymore about them before or after my release.

Chapter 5

In late summer, Pomerania was slowly being filled with the Polish nationals. Mother and the children were dealing with a Polish family that was assigned to take over the farm. They wanted immediate possession of the land and the Polish people and the Russian soldiers harassed them when they returned home from work after dark. The German people were becoming less and less as they were removed from their lands. The German people called the land re-allocation, "Dunkelheit", The Darkness. They were better off than most, the supervising White Russian had previously lived in Germany for many years. They were not treated too badly by the local land grabbers or the immediate Russian supervisors, but when their boss came, they were shouted at, cursed, and ever-so-often, beaten. My family on the farm now consisted of Grandfather, Grandmother, Mother, Elfriede, Siegfried and

Gisela. Without Father and myself, there was no one to do the hard labor but Mother. Grandfather and Siegfried did what they could at home but Mother had to take care of everything. They gathered what they could for moving. They managed to secure additional clothes to ward off the cold and Mother tried swapping extra food for warmer clothing. There was none to be found. The layering clothes were heavy. Many of our possessions were hidden earlier, but suitable clothing was not found.

    Mother saw that the liquid in the septic tank was very low and the guns were now visible. She was frightened that the Poles would turn them in to the Russians. She kept the Poles occupied in the house while Grandpa pulled the guns out of the tank with a rake. Elfriede and Siegfried wrapped them in burlap bags, put them in a basket, and then buried them in the forest under tree roots. On their return to the farm, Elfriede and Siegfried collected tree roots for

Gulag #7

Grandpa to weave into baskets for a cover story, in case they would be asked.

They developed a skin condition. They called it "The Russian Scratch." The skin itched, turned into blisters that burst open to spread the affliction. It looked infectious, always wet and sore. It was very uncomfortable, but not too painful. Elfriede could not work because her hand and fingers were bound together.

A farmer, Leo Walter, who used to live in our village, had come home. He had been drafted into the *Volkssturm* along with father. He brought greetings father and others. He told them that the three avoided capture by the Russians, by going into Schleswig-Holstein by ship, via Denmark, where they were taken prisoner by the British and kept in POW camps until released. They were supposed to work on farms in the vicinity of Meppen (Elmsland).

In October 1945, our neighbor Emil Stiewe was visited by his daughter Leni from Berlin. She brought news of the fathers of Elfriede and Elli Schulzke living and working in Berlin. The three girls, Elfriede, Leni and Elli decided to go to Berlin to find the two fathers. They arrived at the crowded train station on 1 November 1945 when the German expulsion from East Germany was at its peak. The railroad station was filled to the brim with people. They found out that the Polish authorities had gone from house to house to expel all the Pomeranian Germans from their homes; they were then supposed to be resettled in Germany. They knew that time was short and there was no going back home.

They found passage in a cattle car that had no bathroom facilities. They also learned that travel for Germans was restricted. When ever the train came to one of its frequent stops, the Polish people would mob the train cars to take everything they wanted, even clothes off the people's backs and shoes from their feet. One woman called out to Elfriede to help her because she feared that she might lose her children. She could not get through the crowd to help her.

The next day they made their way to a refugee camp on Greeifswalder Street in Berlin where they were given a meal and powdered for lice. Elfriede had been infested with lice from the crowded train and welcomed the insecticide. They went to the Töpfer family home in Berlin. Their house was not destroyed and they met the Grandfather still living there. He had a letter from Father with his return address. In the letter they also found that Leni's father was with him. They were working until they could travel home. The girls did not have travel papers, but a friend arranged for them to acquire whatever documentation was needed. Berlin was divided into four sections. The border between East and West Germany was rapidly closing and they had to hurry if they were to rejoin their families.

The train stopped at the border and they had to walk to Friedland to register for travel, get a meal, and another dosing for lice. They crossed the border and traveled to Ahlorn where the DRK (The German Red Cross) provided them with another warm meal. Elfriede still had the Russian Scratch, but it now covered her body and legs. She said that she looked like a seriously injured person.

They sat at the train station and Elfriede was lucky enough to retain her luggage, that held a thin mattress and bedding that was carried on her back. She also carried a duffel bag that contained food items, mostly bread and grease, but also a little cooked chicken. She wore all the clothes she had. They had missed their connecting train because they fell asleep. They were dead tired and could not stay awake. They woke and took a later train to their stop. From there they had to walk to a single farm house where they had just slaughtered a cow and invited us in for a meal of fresh hamburger. It was delicious. They were taken to the next farm where their fathers worked.

They were greeted kindly but Father Lawrenz was not there. He had injured his hand and could not perform the hard farm labor, so he was out guarding the cattle. The daughter Maria ran out to the field to tell my father that Elfriede was there. Seeing Elfriede, Father wept. It was 15 November 1945, and now she could go home to tell the family that everyone was alive, even if I was not with them.

In the meantime, our relatives from Jannewitz had been expulsed. The Polish family was now living in Elfriede's bedroom. Everyone shared the kitchen and ate their meals in the living room. On 7 November, at 7 a.m., armed men came to the front door ordering my mother and the family from the house. "You have 5 minutes to leave the house. The children and old people have 10 minutes to leave the house."

Mother woke the children and the grandparents and told them to get dressed.

Mother gathered clothing, bedding and what little money they had. The Polish family mother brought food for them to eat on the road. "Grandmother struggled with her paralysis and shouted to the armed men, "I do not want to go. You can shoot me. You can shoot me dead." A horse and wagon was brought to the front of the house and loaded with Grandmother and all their belongings.

The gloves and shoes were missed in the rush to pack and leave. Siegfried returned to the house to get them and when he returned the men hit him. They were told to go to the Schlawer station in Jannewitz to meet with the other expulsed families. There they were load onto railroad cars. They did not know where they were being taken. Some Polish people entered the car and forcibly took what they wanted. The women were bothered, abused and some even killed.

Mother and the family were assigned a room in a house owned by a Stelter family, in Bellin, a small village on a large lake. Food was rationed and Mother had to beg for corn and bread.

Near the end of November 1945, the family went to Berlin to look for Father and Elfriede. They were going to see the Töpfer family, relatives where Elfriede was to stop in her search for Father. In the early morning, they arrived at their relative's home. Mrs. Töpfer answered the door followed by a happy reunion. With a wave of her hand, she directed their attention to the next room where father was lying on a bed. He had just arrived a few days earlier from Meppen. Now all the family was present, except for me, Karl.

Now that they were re-united, they returned to Bellin where Papa immediately found work as a forester. Grandfather wove baskets which they bartered for food. Even with money being earned, there was little food to buy. Food became scarcer by the week. Mrs. Potter helped as much as she could with the little food she had. Her husband was taken by the Russians and either imprisoned or killed. As the food situation worsened, so did my Grandmothers mental health. She became confused and her memory deteriorated. Father and Siegfried decided to try stealing potatoes from the Russians in the neighboring town of Vogelsang. They stole sacks of potatoes without getting caught by stealthy travel through the forest.

Siegfried took up ice sailing on the frozen lake. It was a local popular sport. Elfriede was staying at her uncle Schnelte's house recuperating from her hand injury. Hearing of their food problems in a letter made Elfriede feel sad. Elfriede gave Mrs. Schnelte the letter to read. She immediately sent a letter to my Father, telling him to bring the family to live. She said that she had space and food for them.

Gulag #7

In February 1946 plans were made to move from Bellin to live with the Schneltes. Grandmother was too sick to travel and Grandfather was showing his age, so they decided to go to a retirement home in Uchermunde.

The director of the retirement home returned Grandmother's shoes and Grandfather's long jacket to the family, saying that they had everything needed there for them. Mother traded the shoes for pails of potatoes. Lieschen Krause became severely ill with hunger induced typhoid and died shortly thereafter. She was buried the day before Mother and Father left for Varloh.

An overflowing train of fleeing Germans was taken to the west. Belongings were minimal in order to ease the crossing. The food had almost run out. Mother still had two slices of bread. She divided them up except for a half a slice for the next day. A Russian sat across the aisle and was listening to the conversation. He took his ration of bread and broke off half which he gave to

Gisela. Siegfried the others did not receive any of the bread, but they were happy anyway that Gisela got some food.

The border between East and West Germany was closed and carefully guarded. Crossing the border had to be done at night under dark clouds. The border crossing was successful at the village of Friedland where they registered, received a meal and was powdered for lice. Salve and anti-biotic were also given for our sores.

On 23 March 1946 they arrived at the Schneltes in Varloh, one day before Elfriede's 18th birthday. The family was thin and worn out from lack of food and the arduous trip. The first meal was a banquet of fried potatoes with especially tasteful pieces of bacon. Living space was tight. The Schneltes also had two career English soldiers as a boarders.

Father was working again as a forester and the good meals with his work brought back his health and strength. The rest of the family was

Gulag #7

slowly recovering. We were happy to be where we were, but everything was different and we had to acclimate to our new environment.

They were offered an old school house, 18' x 20' in the village of Varloh that had stood empty for years. They happily accepted the offer. Maria Schneltes canvassed all the inhabitants of the village for extra household items for use by the Lawrenz family. Two beds, a table, chairs, a potbelly stove, dishes, pots, pans, cutlery and a kerosene lamp (there was no electricity). Schneltes gave them a clock to hand on the wall. At first it did not keep time, but ran correctly after being hung. They moved in on 12 April 1946. The school bell still hung above the building and by custom, it was rung every noon.

Mother gave Elfriede Grandmothers jacket that was worn at her wedding in January 1888. Elfriede wore the jacket until it became too small to fit her. After hanging in her closet for years, it was given away. Later Elfriede became mad at herself because the jacket was the last belonging of Grandmothers she had. We were always very close since we grew up with them. Grandmother died on 14 July and Grandfather 27 July 1946

Chapter 6

Prison Camp #7 was surrounded and partitioned in half with high barbed wire fences. There were four guard towers, one at each corner, manned day and night. A training ground for tanks and military exercises surrounded our camp. One day I recognized my aunt, the wife of my mother's brother, on the women's side of a fence. We waved to each other and were observed by a guard. The women were immediately moved back away from the fence, and a wider separation was established between the two groups. A sanitation "Privy" building straddled the fence line separating the women's side from the men. The two sides shared the same pit. We sat with a horizontal pole beneath our knees and leaned against the wall made of mesh wire. Usually we had newspaper for wiping, and sometimes not.

Charles Schwend

After the first two months in camp #7, more than half of the 900 prison population died from diarrhea and other illnesses brought on by the living conditions. Five of which were my close friends. The dead bodies were undressed before being thrown into a holding bunker until they could be put into a mass grave. A guard with 4 prisoners was taken before noon to dig a grave 8'x8'x5'. It took all day to dig a grave deep enough. By dark, we would get a hay frame wagon, pushing it by hand to the bunker, to load the bodies from both the men's and woman's camp. The bodies were so decomposed, the skin slipped off the flesh when lifting them. One woman's body was so bad, I had to turn away and throw up. Taking the wagon to the mass grave we dug, the bodies were thrown in and covered with dirt. Once, an arm stuck up out of the ground from rigor mortis. A guard took a spade and chopped the arm off in order to cover the bodies with dirt.

Gulag #7

A typical guard tower of a Gulag in Siberia

Chapter 7

Two prisoners escaped from the camp. No one I knew was aware of the circumstances, or when it took place, but it caused a big ruckus with the guards. We were asked a lot of questions of how, when and where. The guards told us that they would find then, and they did two days later. They had the two escapees on a truck and paraded them past us before throwing them to the ground in front of us. They were beaten and bloody. Guards took them to a discipline bunker and we heard sounds of more beatings. We were told the escapees did not survive and were later thrown into the dead body holding bunker for later mass burial. Rumor had it that they were planning to flee across Siberia and swim to Alaska.

My aunt survived Prison Camp #7 after working in a coalmine for five years before being released, blind and unable to continue working.

Gulag #7

She passed away at the age of 88 years. Some of my fellow prisoners were also sent to the coal mines and many did not come back.

All the able Russian men were in the military and the Russian woman were assigned to many of the laborious jobs. One day while we were on road repair detail, we encountered these women unloading railroad coal cars. They jeered us, making fun of who and what we were, calling out to flirt and proposition us in a very demeaning manner. Some of the words they said made me blush

Our daily routine started with an early shrill awakening at 6 a.m. Breakfast at 6:30. We were taken to our work detail at 7:00, then return to camp at 6:30 p.m. We were given dinner at 7:30 and our lights were out at 11:p.m. All of our meals were ate in the barracks, but prepared somewhere else. Some of the weaker were too tired to respond to the wake-up alarm and were beat with rubber clubs. Some labored in the coal mine while others worked on a farm or road construction. The farms were all owned by the state and worked with prisoner labor. We were never allowed to be near the women and I do not know what kind of work they were forced to do, but I can imagine their life was equally hard. We buried many of them from the dead holding bunker.

Our daily food regimen consisted of a thin soup of water, and noodles or cabbage, and green tomatoes with a small piece of bread. I can not, or will not, say what we called this watered down liquid, but on more than one occasion someone would say, "Hey, I think I found a noodle in my can," or "What is this, a bean?" On rare occasions we had dried and salted herring. We rubbed the fish vigorously to remove as much salt as possible. A lot of water was needed to wash down the high concentration of salt in the fish. On other rare occasions we were treated with some kind of pigeon that was followed the next day with soup.

Gulag #7

We picked the leaves from weeds for salads. We could also carry the dead bodies for an extra ration, a can of soup. Even with all this 'good food' my weight plummeted to 87 lbs.

Once in a while we would get a little tobacco to be rolled up in Russian newspaper that we would smoke to repel mosquitoes. Sometimes I would trade my tobacco for a little pat of butter. The Russian guards would carry their tobacco loose in their pocket with Russian newspaper, never German newspaper, because they felt the Russian paper was superior and smoked better. They said, "Russian paper is made from wood, who knows what the German paper is made of."

Chapter 8

After World War II ended, the food became a little better, but I ended in a hospital for about a week with a bad case of pneumonia, an illness that killed many of my co-internees. I spent the next two weeks resting with a light work schedule. We were driven to a farm where we cut cabbage heads in half, threw them into a silo and walked barefooted around and over them to break the heads down. The silo was then closed up to ferment the cabbage into sauerkraut. This was supposed to make a better kraut. We were also given "Kascha" a dessert salad made with plain sauerkraut and green tomatoes, another food that promoted the deadly diarrhea. Gruel made of wheat, barley or rye, or a sauerkraut soup was also given to us.

Once, we were walking through a small town to a work site and school children lined the road shouting, "Hitler Kaputt", "Germany

Kaputt". The children surrounded us with our guard's approval, cutting off any shiny buttons for souvenirs to keep.

Two weeks after my discharge from the hospital, I was sent to a farm where we repaired roads and built homes. Actually, they were huts, made with birch tree poles stuck vertically into the ground and smaller birch branches woven horizontally between the poles. We made a plaster of mud and straw, mixed by walking horses in it until a suitable consistency was reached. Then we chinked and plaster the woven walls and struck off the walls flat with a board, followed by a type of paint. Inside, bricklayers built a large oven. The completed hut looked rather luxurious compared to what we were use to.

Our living quarters on the farm was an old sheep barn or machine shed that was built solid. It was dark when we first arrived, and the guard, told us not to turn on any lights. He caught birds that were nesting in the rafters and twisted off their heads. He built a fire, then after packing the bird carcasses in mud, threw them into the fire. After the mud cracked open, he pulled them from the fire with a stick. He showed us how to pull the mud away with the feathers, to feed on the baked meat. This is one of the ways we supplemented our meager rations.

Around fifty prisoners slept in the structure, on straw that was strewn on the ground for the sheep. The sheep summered in the wilderness and returned to their barn for the winter. One night during the midnight sun, July or August, we were awakened by our guard and told to come outside. He wanted to treat us to the midnight sun. The sun did not set, just dropped to follow the horizon before returning back up. He read his newspaper with this midnight sunlight, while watching us. You could plainly read by the light of the sun riding on the horizon. By this time we were in rags. We were given the clothes

Gulag #7

from the dead, since they did not need them anymore. The soles separated from my shoes and I had wrapped wire around them to hold the soles on.

Another prison camp lay within eyesight of where we were interned. The prisoners were Russian soldiers that disobeyed their orders; not be captured alive. They were brought from German POW camps and taken to Siberia where they were re-interned. They existed in conditions less than we had. I think none of them survived.

In September 1945 we were informed to prepare ourselves for a trip back to Germany. Before we left, a fellow prisoner stopped me to give me his coat, telling me, "I will never make it home, after being underfed and sleeping on bare boards." Opening his shirt, he showed me his black and blue body. He insisted on giving me his coat. I could not refuse. Later, I found 10 German Marks in the pocket. The generous man died two days later. His death was very hard on me.

I was scheduled to be in the first train back to East Germany because of being so underweight and weak. The Doctor, a German, told me, "Karl, you would not endure the four to five weeks trip by train to East Germany. You should stay her for at least two more weeks to get better before trying to travel that distance and for that amount of time. I know that many healthy people do not make it back alive."

We were allowed to leave the boxcars at stops, to exercise and stretch our legs. On one of these stops, I must have strayed too far and got a strange feeling in the pit of my stomach. There was no warning whistle before the train started pulling out. I was weak from the diet of little food, but managed to throw myself on the car coupler. It took me awhile to pull myself fully onto the coupler and there I had to sit and rest. The effort completely wore me out. It was all I could do to sit and hang on. Many times I have thought, "Karl, where did you get the strength?" I feel the Lord grabbed me by the pants and threw me up onto the coupler. At the next stop, I did not walk around, but went straight to my car. My fellow train companions thought I was lost, never expecting my return and were surprised to see me.

On the trip, we slowly rolled through the Russian capital, "Moscow". The train station was clean, full of glitter and shine. We were told that the columns were made of marble and decorated with gold paint.

Before reaching the 'new' Polish border, we were informed that the Polish people were extremely hateful toward the Germans. Our box car doors were closed and locked before getting to the Poland. While traveling through Poland, our cars were pelted with rocks, sticks or anything available to throw. No one was hurt, but we all had terrible feelings on being threatened on what was our original homeland. We had to cluster in the middle of the box car floor to avoid being struck by small projectiles coming through the cracks between the wall boards.

We were loaded into boxcars, maybe the same ones that brought us to Siberia. Instead of 80 people to a boxcar, we were now only 40 in each. Also, the food was better and whenever the train stopped, we were allowed to get out and exercise ourselves. At every stop there was a market or vendors selling produce and other foods. They were expensive and we did not have the money. On one occasion at a stop, a Russian woman approached me, put her arms around me and said, "Oh, you poor little boy," and gave me 10 rubles from her pocket. I bought a water glass of sunflower seeds. Her kindness gave me a big boost and a new physical and mental start.

Up to this point, I was so bitter toward the Russian people. I would ask myself, *"What have I done to deserve this, I should be home with my family. I am only 15 years old."*

Gulag #7

Later on the trip, our train was put on a side rail for a more important train to pass. One of the women prisoners, a young good looking girl, was relieving herself under a car of another side railed train. There was a whistling and she tried to get out from under the train, but it jerked and she lost both legs above the knee. I do not know what happened to her after that. I think she was just left there to bleed to death. After five weeks we arrived at Frankfurt, by the river Oder. We were told that we could not return to our home in Pomerania. The Polish people had taken our land.

Chapter 9

So, what to do? My friend Hans and I, the same age, sixteen, and around ninety pounds, bummed around and decided we should travel to Berlin, East Germany. We looked like twins, both with light brown hair, same build and the same height. We traveled by train, sleeping in or on the train and bus terminals. In Berlin, we begged for food on street corners or at houses, or even ate out of garbage cans. We also help ourselves to the many vegetable gardens. We were caught helping ourselves to potatoes and the police were called. We were arrested and taken to the police station where we ate our first 'real' meal since being removed from home.

The Chief of Police found us a job at a Russian Army Station in New Strelitz, a part of East Berlin. I cleaned and groomed the horses, fed and cared for their livestock, which the Russian Soldiers had stolen from the farmers. A cow or a pig a week was killed. We would take the meat from the slaughter house and bread from the bakery to the Russian mess. We did get plenty to eat, which helped me gain some weight and get my strength back.

I remember Christmas on the farm. There were eight people working there. On Christmas Eve, after all the chores were done, we gathered in the living room. We had a tree decorated with candles. After re-arranging all the decorations, the lights were turned out. Off in a corner, someone would start singing Stille Nacht, Heilige Nacht "Silent Night, Holy Night", and everyone would join in. The singing was followed with tearful eyes. There was not a dry eye in the group. After wishing everyone a Merry Christmas, we hugged, and went our own way.

On occasion, I drove the Russian Commandant through the countryside in a carriage. He was looking for young German girls for entertainment. The job lasted three months, until all the animals were butchered. With no more work available for us, we were released. Later I found work at a calcium plant where we dug the calcium with spades, laying it on the ground to dry. The calcium was ground and used as an additive to cement, or for whitewashing buildings. Wages were small and I could not buy anything with the small amount of money I was paid. I received food stamps, but there was very little you could purchase with them. All this time I was trying to locate my family.

My father who was captured on the Western Front, was now released from the allied POW camp, came to Berlin looking for the family, as did my sister. She was living in Swenemuende, where my grandparents were buried, North of Berlin. I had contacted the Red Cross after I remembered the names and addresses of relatives. After several attempts to locate anyone related to me, I finally received a positive answer and was informed that my relatives were able to return to their homes.

My family had been trying to locate me while I was searching for them. I now lived in New Strelitz near Berlin. My relatives had gotten word to me that my family lived in Varloh, County of Meppen in northwestern Germany. I immediately wrote my parents and received a reply within two weeks, telling me to come home where the whole family was waiting for me. Hans stayed in New Strelitz.

There was a large obstacle to my returning; the border between East and West Germany was closed. A legal visa was required to pass through the border. Friends of mine told me that people with no visa would just run across the border. Fine, I thought I would try that and bought a train ticket to the boarder. Five miles before we reached the border, the train stopped and the border patrol asked for my visa. I was asked to leave the train when I could not produce one. I then decided to walk to the boarder to attempt a crossing.

I had walked about 20km until I neared the border. I was scared and hid in a rye field. When I stood up again to walk toward the border a man was standing off in the distance. He waved to me to come closer. When I approached him he stopped me and said, "You look like you need help." I just knew Jesus sent him to me. I think he lived in that small town that straddled the border. I told him my story and my current visa problem. I also showed him my mother's letter. He advised me to go to the barracks in front of us and tell one of the men my story and where I wanted to go. I went to the barracks and talked to the first man I met. He took me to the man in charge.

Everyone there was waiting to cross the border. The man in charge owned a flat wagon that was used daily to haul a group of people across the border. Horses were not allowed in no-mans-land, so we had to push the wagon. There was a Russian guard at the entrance to no-mans-land checking documentation. I tried to stand behind a larger man, and not be noticeable. The guard said O.K. "caresho" and waved us all through.

Chapter 10

That day I crossed the border to West Germany, in Friedland, the little town that straddled the border. I was welcomed by the Red Cross and other officials at a stand that welcomed all the people crossing the border and received a good meal, a sandwich and a cup of hot chocolate. I was then put into an adjacent refugee camp to stay overnight where I was given more food. With the letter showing a relatives address from my mother, I received a train ticket to Geesto, County of Meppen that was paid for by the government. Transportation was authorized by my release papers from prison camp #7 and endorsed at Frankfurt, Oder. From there I had to walk barefooted to the town of Varloh, about 16 KM from the train station.

Gulag #7

Top: 1946 – My Family at Varloh. Bottom: Front of our house with lean-to for piglets and tools. The bell was rung daily at noon as a religious custom.

Slowly life normalized for my family in Varloh. In the spring of 1946 they planted their first garden in land loaned from the Schneltes. A shed was built for firewood and some chickens. Varloh was too small for a grocery store, so Mother would travel to Meppen to shop. She took a path through a pasture and past a refuge dump where she would scavenge for useful items. Cans, pails and pots were usually found. Sometimes useful pieces of cloth were picked up. Everything found had a use in our sparse household.

The letter my family received from me in April was a joyful event for them, even after I informed them of my illness that was holding me back from coming home. I had been released from the prison camp and making my way home after receiving their address from the Potter family.

Finally, I arrived at my parent's home in the afternoon of June 6th, 1946, my mother's birthday. The welcome I received from my family and friends was beyond explanation. From February 1945 until June 6th 1946, I was separated from my family. I took my first bath in over a year. All my clothes were burned because they were riddled with holes and infested with lice and other biting bugs. Mother made me a pair of trousers from a blanket.

My weight was down to 89lbs. For several weeks at home, my mother tried to bulk me up with whatever food she could find. Even then in 1946, food was scarce and groceries could not be bought without food stamps. I applied for and was given work on a farm; the best place to get food.

Siegfried was slowly recovering from a stomach disorder caused by malnourishment. He was eating small meals four or five times a day. Food was still rationed, but more was available for purchase. Our financial situation improved enabling us to buy a cook stove and proper cooking utensils. A cellar was dug and the stable expanded. Pigs and a rabbit were purchased and fed with garden scraps

Elfriede's hands were improving and she started to knit and sew. She also started helping outside. She received a spring dress for the warming weather. In November 1946 Elfriede received training as a spinner and found work in the firm Nino. She and other girls that finished the training stayed at the home of one of the girl's mother. In January 1947 the girls moved to the company barracks with other girls. Their dorm held eleven girls in nice beds.

The clothing situation at home was still a problem. Father and I had three pairs of trousers between us. Elfriede brought material from her work to make us two more pair.

My friend Walter and I played on a soccer team in a Sunday afternoon league. My team held a mid range standing. The name of the team was, and still is, SV Schwefingen.

Gulag #7

After the game we were looking for something more exciting to do. We ate, went to a movie, and then learned of a dance on the outskirts of the neighboring town Meppen that is about the size of Springfield, Illinois. The dance was being held in a newly built hall. We decided a dance was a good thing to do. Arriving, we found the music great, and the girls beautiful. Introducing myself, I secured a dance partner, Erica, and invited her and her friend to join Walter and myself at our table.

It was past midnight when the last dance call was announced. After the finale, I asked Erica if she had a bicycle to which she said "No." I started to walk her home, pushing my bike until I asked her if she would like a ride. "I can take you home." I said. She replied, "Yes."

On the way to her home, we had to cross over a bridge where a Police Officer was stationed. He stopped us and informed me that it was against the law for two people to ride on the same bike. I was fined 1 Mark. I paid the fine, thanking the officer, and we continued on – walking – until we were out of the officer's sight. Erica got back on the bike and we continued

on our way to her house. We could see the dawn lighting the sky in the East and we both had to work that day. We enjoyed some hugs and a final kiss, when Erica said, "Sweetheart, you better go home. My husband is coming home any moment now." I picked up my bike from the south corner of the house and gave a final wave goodbye when I saw a young man leaning his bike on the other side of the house. This was the first and last time I ever saw Erica, but keep her always in my memories.

In 1948, the German Mark was devaluated to 10% of its value. The new currency was called 'Deutsche Mark (DM). After the devaluation, food stamps were no longer required. Everything on the market was open for purchase. I left the farm and found a job at an oil refinery, where my first job was on the ground crew. We dug ditches for the oil pipes, and then laying the pipe, followed by insulating the pipe with cloth and tar. Later I built roads and accesses to the pumps.

Standing security at my post in the Oil Refinery - 1958

The last 5 years I was a security guard. An old friend recommended me for the security post after working as a mail delivery man and 'gofer' in the office building. I inspected the trucks going in and out, for anything unusual. Also, directing telephone calls and visitors was part of my duties. Visitors had to be escorted to the office complex by an authorized person. During the evening swing shift, I passed the time by reading. During this time I enjoyed dancing, movies and playing soccer.

On 18 July 1950, my sister Elfriede married Horst Kubeit in the Gustav-Adolf church in Schwefingen village. As was the custom, they were driven to the church in a carriage. She was dressed in white and the groom in a beautiful dark suit.

I lived 5 miles from the refinery and commuted on a bicycle. In the winter my bike had to be carried by me through the heavier snow, usually bringing about a very cold sweat that aggravated my lungs. In 1952 I again came down with pneumonia and my doctor placed me in a

T.B. clinic, where I was treated with a lot of rest and medicine, calcium pills I think. The doctor told me that the pneumonia caused dark shadows on my lungs, just like T.B. and was treated as such.

In April 1952 brother Siegfried completed his education in the printing business. His successful completion of the final examination was satisfying and relieving for our parents.

On 3 November 1952 Mother and Father celebrated their Silver Anniversary in Varloh. They had expanded their house, giving them additional living space and installing electricity was in the process.

Chapter 11

Top - Inge and myself when engaged
Bottom - My wife Inge and myself at Christmas

Inge's and Karl's Engagement Party – Sept 1953

While recuperating in the T.B. clinic I met a beautiful girl, Inge Driesner. She was originally a patient at the clinic, then after being cured, became a nursing student. After graduating from her training she took a position as a staff nurse. She was originally from Linde, Provence Gerdauen, East Prussia, where they raised Trakehner horses. We were engaged in

September 1953. We were married October 30, 1954, at Inge's parent's home, in Wittmond near Aurich Germany.

Wedding Day October 30, 1954

We honeymooned at Inge's parent's house. They fixed up a spare bedroom for us. It held a rickety bed, no mattress, just springs with a cover over it. The center of the springs was held up with an old ammunition box. I had a lot of serious thoughts about that ammo box during that first night. Later we moved to Dalum, and rented a 2nd floor apartment from one of my friends, near the county seat of Meppen, where I still worked at the oil refinery. On March 14th, 1957, our first daughter, Marita was born, followed by our second, Karin on October 5^{th,} 1958.

In November 1954 Papa became ill with Pleurisy. He laid 15 weeks in the hospital before coming down with Bronchial asthma. He could no longer work and had to go onto retirement pension early.

Papa had hoped to get the home in Jannewitz back, but gave up any hope of it. He then decided to build in Varloh. He received a small amount of compensation for the land taken over by the Polish and the retirement pension, and applied that to building their new home. Construction started on 20 September and was finished by 20 December 1957. At Christmas the Lawrenz family had a double celebration. In April 1958 Siegfried successfully completed examination for a Masters Craftsman Diploma. He then made a practical application of his learning in building himself a new home.

In December 1958, Inge's parents and family immigrated to the United States. There were housing problems in Germany from all the people that left the lands taken over by the polish and forced to move from East to West Germany. The overpopulation strained the housing available. The oil wells were going dry and I was about to lose my job.

In light of my job loss and the scarcity of housing, we discussed the possibility of trying to follow Inge's parents to the USA. We prayed for help from the Lord in making our big decision. Immigration to the United States was complicated and needed careful thought. We wrote to Inge's parents, explaining what we were thinking about. We had their answer and advice in a short while. The Sunday School Class at the First Baptist Church, in Highland Illinois would take on the

Gulag #7

responsibility of sponsorship for us. Clinton Rogier, a member of this class assumed the role of actual sponsor. Through the "World Council of Churches" help we applied for a Visa for immigration. All the documentation was completed so quick it made my head spin.

Visa Interview at the U.S. Embassy at Hamburg- 1959

We were scheduled to leave Germany on December 14, 1959. We had little time for
116

preparation. We had to sell all our furniture and anything else we could not take with us. I made a wooden box to send important items by ship. This shipment arrived in Highland about four weeks after reaching our new home.

In December 1959, my brother Siegfried took us to the train station in Meppen for the trip to Munich. We departed from Munich the next day when we had to say goodbye to our loved ones, friends and family, not knowing if we will ever see each other again. There were no dry eyes and I can still see mom and dad standing there waving to us as we left. The flight was good. We had good meals, with Christmas music, in Iceland and Newfoundland and both airports were covered in snow. We had enough room on the aircraft to spread out a blanket for the children for napping and to change diapers. The aircraft we were in was an older DC3 and very vulnerable to dropping in air pockets. We had not experienced this before and it felt like our stomachs would come up out of our mouths. This was also extremely troublesome when using the toilet. I had feared that it would have the effect of using a bidet. We arrived in New York, after flying 24 hours, to see bright sunshine.

Upon landing, a lady translator introduced herself to us as our escort and welcomed us to the United States. We walked to a waiting bus to take us to the train station. We exchanged our money to U.S. dollars. We had trouble getting the vending machines to work but it seemed there was always someone around to help. Everyone was so friendly and helpful. Our escort made us familiar with our train, showing us the dining room and told us that at the end of every car there were restrooms.

Our seats were reversible and were very comfortable, just like sitting in an easy chair at home. The sleeping accommodations were also very comfortable. We each were given a blanket for the trip, but they had to be left on the train when we departed. Our two girls showed their good manners and upbringing during the trip. We were only on the train for 22 hours.

In Germany, all the restrooms are unisex, like on airplanes. I could not read or write English and when I first had to use the restroom, I stopped to watch for people going in and coming out a door. I did not notice that only women were using the door I was watching. I casually opened the door to screams and cursing. I found out that there are not unisex restrooms in the United States. I was pointed to the direction of the next door. I was met by waiters with white towels draped over their forearm and was greeted with a welcome to the dining room. This was not what I was expecting, or wanted, so I turned around and walked out. Another try was taken and I finally found the correct door. I considered myself lucky to have finally found my urgent destination in time.

I met two U.S. Soldiers that were also going to St. Louis. They tried to make me understand NOT to get off the train in East St. Louis. They held onto me until the train left East St. Louis. "No, East St. Louis. Yes, St. Louis." At the train station, Inge's parents, her brother Mannfred and our sponsor, Clinton Rogier, met us.

We traveled by train to St. Louis, Missouri. Travel in the U.S. was not the best, not speaking English and we held the two girls on our laps to keep them quiet and calm. We arrived in St. Louis on December 16th, 1959 at the old Union Station, then two hours later, arrived in Highland, IL, with bright sunlight, a beautiful sight to see. We were taken to our new home at 800 Laurel St. It was a very warm day for December, but that was tempered later that winter when we had the worst weather I've ever experienced in Highland.

Chapter 12

We had a warm welcome from the members of the First Baptist Church, with lots of presents of beds, household items and a refrigerator. The next two months I worked on my ex-brother-in-law, Jonathan Rogier's farm. In 1967 I became a naturalized citizen and changed my name to Karl Heinz Lawrenz. I also registered for the Selective Service on 4-11-1967.

On March7th, 1960, I started working at Basler Electric earning $1.65 per hour setting up the motor winding machines. It was rough for me at work because I still did not speak English well. It did not take long for me to understand almost everything I needed to know for working at Basler Electric. From then on it was full steam ahead. By the end of 1969, I was promoted to group leader for the motor coil winding department and early in 1972 I was again promoted to shop foreman.

Gulag #7

In May 1960, I located my Uncle Ernest Lawrenz, who is my Fathers Brother. He immigrated to the USA in 1920. My Uncle Ernest and wife Marguerite lived in St. Petersburg, Florida. They loaned us $7,500 to purchase the home we still live in.

The first time I ever stepped into a high school was when my brother-in-law Manfred Driesner graduated from the Highland High School. During the ceremony there was an announcement over the public address system, stating my name and that I had a visitor. There waiting for me at the main door were my uncle Ernest and his wife. After this meeting we continued to visit each other until they passed away.

A group of visiting VIP's, engineers and plant owners from Germany came for a tour of Baslers. I was asked by management to serve as their host. They had their own interpreters, but I still translated some of the technical aspects peculiar to this plant, explaining the different department functions. We finished the tour over a fine meal at Michael's Restaurant. During the time as shop foreman, I traveled for the company throughout the U.S. and Mexico teaching quality control methods. In September 1994, I retired from Basler Electric at age 65.

My last day of work at Basler Electric

I could not just sit around, so I took a position at the First Baptist Church in Highland,

Gulag #7

as their janitor, that I held until 1989, when I had a heart attack. A quadruple by-pass was performed on me. In 2001 I applied for and received a position as a greeter at the Highland Wal-Mart.

My first car was a Buick Roadmaster. Otto Riggs, the sales manager at the 4-5-6 Buick dealership, said they only built one hundred like mine with three holes in the front fender. All the rest has four holes.

Uncle Ernest, myself and my Buick Roadmaster

Since then we have made several trips to visit my Uncle Ernest and have enjoyed vacations in Minnesota; Wisconsin Dells; Pidgin Ford, Tennessee; and Branson, Missouri. We have traveled back to Germany several times and visit our daughter Marita in Burlington, Ontario, Canada, each year.

Gulag #7

The back of our old home in Jannewitz. 1992 Photo shows the current Polish resident who rents it from the Polish government.

Front of our house in Jannewitz – 1992.

In 1977, our daughter Marita married Ben Bennink in Canada. They have five children, three girls and two boys. In 1979 our Daughter Karin married David Jacober. They have three boys. They divorced in 1996.

On June 16, 2001, Karin re-married to Patrick McMullen, and is very happy. He is an accomplished handy man, an engineer by education and working at Basler Electric. He helped me remodel my entire home, including all new wiring and plumbing. Karin is a Teller at First Mid Illinois & Trust in Highland, IL.

In 1972 I had a hernia operation, in 1989 I had a heart attach and was taken to the St. Johns hospital in Springfield, IL, for an angioplasty surgery. In 1995 I had a back surgery on my spinal cord at St. Luke's hospital in St. Louis, Mo. And in 1999 I had a quadruple bypass. Up until now I am doing real well, doing some volunteer work in the community and at the First Baptist Church, the same church that brought our family to this wonderful city. At the end of 1999 I had another surgery for corporal tunnel on my right hand.

In 2001 I started working at Wal-Mart in Highland, IL. And up to this day, I am still working there.

In August of 2001, my wife Inge and I were shopping in the Big Lots store in Glen Carbon. I was shopping for a greeting card and Inge was just browsing. Inge called out from the other side of the shelving. "Karl, come quick." Going around the shelving I saw a younger woman holding her mother. She was crying for help and crying out, "Mom, please don't die." I quickly grabbed the elderly woman to keep her from falling and laid her on the floor. Checking her vital signs I realized she did not have a pulse. Remembering my CPR training I starting the resuscitation work. She had blood coming from her mouth but soon began to softly moan. The daughter told me her mother had regained her pulse. By this time the E.M.T. had arrived and hooked up their monitors, then told me that she was stable enough for transport to the hospital. The daughter thanked me for my assistance and followed her mother out to the ambulance. On leaving the store, the clerk asked me for my name and address and I replied that I was already thanked. This reinforcement my belief that first aid and CPR training is very important.

Postscript

My sister Elfriede Kubeit is widowed and living in Nordhorn, Germany, and my other sister Gisela also lives in Nordhorn with her husband Joseph Zelle. My brother Siegfield and his wife Hanna live in Varloh, County of Meppen, Germany.

My wife Inge died November 6th, 2004, one week after our Golden Wedding Anniversary. Inge's family consisted of 6 girls and 4 boys. Her oldest brother married and stayed in Germany. Her family also had to leave their home and travel to West Germany.

My mother Margarete died on 07-27-1988 in Meppen, Germany.

My father Albert died on 07-12-1992 in Wueneminde, East Germany.

My maternal grandparents: Friedrich Czemper – DOB: 12-21-1879. DOD: 12-21-1914 in Russia.

Bertha Czemper nee Vircus – DOB: 02-14-1882. DOD: 02-17-1969.

My paternal grandparents: Hermann Lawrenz – DOB: 03-27-1865. DOD: 07-27-1946. Albertine Lawrenz nee Weubauer – DOB: 11-23-1967. DOD: 07-14-1946.

This story tells how I started in Germany as a youth in 1929 through my current life in Highland, IL. It is dedicated to my loving family.

Gulag #7

Our Wedding photo.

Charles Schwend

*"Marriage is a promise
to communicate and share,
To treat each other with respect,
to listen and to care,
Marriage is a commitment
by a husband and a wife
To be each other's lover, friend,
and confidant for life."*

This book is dedicated to my lovely wife Inge and family.

With all my love, Karl Lawrenz

The following pages are Bonus material for your enjoyment

Gulag #7

Read the short story

The Good and Bad

A short story from the book

The Keys

And other short stories

Now available at most major book stores, Ebay and Amazon.

Charles Schwend

The Good And Bad

Whomph. Whomph. Whomph.

The man is lost in the darkened woods, running for his life. Something in the sky is pursuing him. Looking over his right shoulder he sees giant wings coming closer. The thing, whatever it is, started following him, just before dusk. Running and evading the flying creature for the last three hours has left him weak, hungry and thirsty. Instinct tells him he will be dead if he stops or tries to hide. The wings beating the air are becoming louder, and closer. The thing starts to dive, picking up speed. He forces himself to try running faster. The wings quietly slice through the air as it slowly descends upon him, like an owl in the wild, striking prey. A spur pushes out from the wing tip joint. A quick slash brings the man to ground. The thing, a human form with large wings, settles down to stand on its prey. Talons are where toes exist on humans, but this is not human.

The talons tear into the man's back, crushing his spine. He screams in agony as bone is yanked from his body. Then with talons locked into his shoulders, is lifted high into the sky. Moments later the man is dropped from one hundred feet onto an outcropping of rock. Bones are shattered. Regaining consciousness, the man has no feeling from his waist down. His arms are broken, and head concussed. He cannot move his head,

Gulag #7

but can rotate his eyes. He can see human bones scattered across the outcropping. They gleam in the moonlight. They are gnawed and crushed. He does not know how long he was unconscious and is fearful of the next few minutes. Something that he cannot see begins chewing on his feet and legs. There is no pain, but he can sense pulling and the tearing of flesh. He hears rustling as something approaches him from behind and he feels painful chewing on his ear. A furry animal, a rat, scurries across his head to begin eating his nose and lips. He squeezes his eyes shut hard, as if to force out the pain. Opening his eyes when he feels a larger furry animal brush past his face, he sees and smells a stinking possum looking back and forth, as if checking for competition to the newfound meal. His mind reels in terror as the possum begins chewing just above his groin. The possum enters his stomach and eats half way up to his throat before the relief of death overcomes him. His last thoughts were regret for killing the picnicking couple in the late afternoon.

His soul, a black oily substance, slowly begins the long painful trip down, through the earth's crust, toward the burning core, where other like souls reside. Some will be vomited up through volcanoes for a teasing, temporary exposure to sunlight, only to be thrown back down for another painful re-passing into the earth's core, surely a punishment for their choice of living existence. Others will be forced up through the ocean bottoms, like hell's defecation, to mix with the slime of the sea life's excretion, before passing again, down to the earth's core.

He had no way of knowing that the larger carnivores of the woodland visited him to eat during the night. Come sunrise, the birds of the forest complete their task of cleansing their environment. The partial skeleton, of mostly crushed and eaten bones, remains bleaching in the bright warm sun.

At next dusk, the winged humanoid begins its nightly patrol. A quiet whimper is heard. Dropping down to the tree top level, eagle like vision detects a small being, not much more than a toddler. Lost, scared and quietly sobbing, he does not know where to go or what to do after his parents were viciously killed the day before. The winged humanoid slowly circles, like a vulture descending to its meal, until landing in front of the small boy. Cooing to relax and comfort, it wraps its wings around the boy with caresses that feel like cascading goose down. Cradling the small human in its arms, the creature takes flight into the night.

Risking detection, it flies over the small town, landing at the side door of a church. Mentally voiding the memories of the small child, he sits him on the step and knocks loudly on the door, interrupting the evening service. A quick take off has it out of sight before the door opens. "My heavens, who are you? Where are you from?" exclaims the usher. Looking around and

Gulag #7

seeing nothing out of the ordinary, the man picks up the child to return to the warmth of the church interior.

    The humanoid watched from hidden safety until assuring himself the child was safe, then again took flight, searching, always searching, for the good and bad, exacting punishment and reward to each it's due. The Angel is always on patrol.

Charles Schwend

Read the Prologue to

The Palace

of Virtual Reality

Now available at most major book stores, Ebay and Amazon.

Gulag #7

Prologue

Somewhere in Ancient Britannia

Oh God, hear my words. Let me die now and not suffer for eternity. I do not deserve to languish in this insufferable hell of darkness and solitude. I have prayed for even the smallest spark of light to postpone the insanity that has befallen me. This blanket of blackest night has stopped time. I know not if my confinement has been days, weeks, months, years, or centuries. My powers have dwindled to nothing. I feel I am nothing more than a memory of a memory.

I was Merlin the Great. I had planned to create a world of peace and happiness, and now I am less than a grain of sand. How could have I been so foolish to let Niviane, the Lady of the Lake, trap and imprison me in this inescapable black vault of rock? She was more beguiling than the sweetest flower until she learned all that I knew. How could I have known what her ulterior motives were, before my sudden betrayal suffered at her hands? Her sinister actions turned my heart cold.

Even now, knowing what I do, with my demise imminent, I feel my actions, my mistakes leading to my present confinement, would only be repeated. As I feel my remaining essence, from the smallest part of my being, slip away, I know that I will be no more. My only consolation is that my manuscript, holding the records of myself and that of all the ancient gods will someday be discovered. Everything about the gods and I, all the physical descriptions and details of mental psyche and design, recorded for the inheritors of the world to view. Maybe then, just maybe, our deeds and thoughts will again enlighten the world.

I am tired of my cruelly imposed existence, and must now relinquish myself to the eternal sleep. I ....

Gulag #7

Read the Crème' de Menthe
Recipe from the book
Homemade Cordials
Better Than Bought

Now available at most major book stores, Ebay and Amazon.

Charles Schwend

Crème de Menthe (1 Fifth)

1 Cup Fresh Mint Leaves

1 Cup 100p Vodka

½ Cup Brandy

1 Cup Honey (or sugar)

2 Cups Water

1 Teaspoon Food Grade Glycerin (for good mouth feel)

2 Drops Green Food Coloring

Rinse, dry and stem mint leaves. Remove any bad spots in the leaf. Different mints will give different flavors. Black Forest mint is the strong mint used in mint patties.
(You can also use the various essential oils of mint instead of the fresh leaves. I recommend adding drops of the essential oil until you achieve the strength you desire.) Tear or chop the leaves into ½ to ¾ in pieces and place in a clean quart canning jar. Pour the vodka and brandy over the leaf pieces. Screw on lid and place in a cool and dark place for at least 8 days. After the 8 days, strain and place liquid into a clean quart canning jar. Combine the sugar and water into a sauce pan to make a simple syrup. Heat over medium heat until the syrup clears, then simmer for 5 minutes (this is to kill any feral yeast that may be

Gulag #7

present in the sugar). Cool until room temperature then pour over mint liquid. Add the glycerin and food coloring. Taste and adjust ingredients to your taste. Screw on lid and place in a cool dark place. Your cordial can be served after 12 to 16 weeks. Place into an appropriate serving bottle, (green would be nice, and facetted to impress your guests), or a fifth bottle. If there is air space below the neck, add a little more vodka or brandy as you desire. A suggestion for a crisp fall evening would be to add this to a cup of hot cocoa.

www.ingramcontent.com/pod-product-compliance
Lightning Source LLC
LaVergne TN
LVHW051605070426
835507LV00021B/2782